The Miracle Dulcimer

27 Easy-to-play Songs for the Mountain Dulcimer & So Much More!

Natalie Buske Thomas

ISBN-13:
978-0966691986
ISBN-10:
0966691989

Dedicated to:

My mother, Joy Lynn

Special Thanks to:

Casey
Jay
Kelly
Hannah
Traci
Howard
Kelli
Rebecca
Paul

AUTHOR'S WORKS

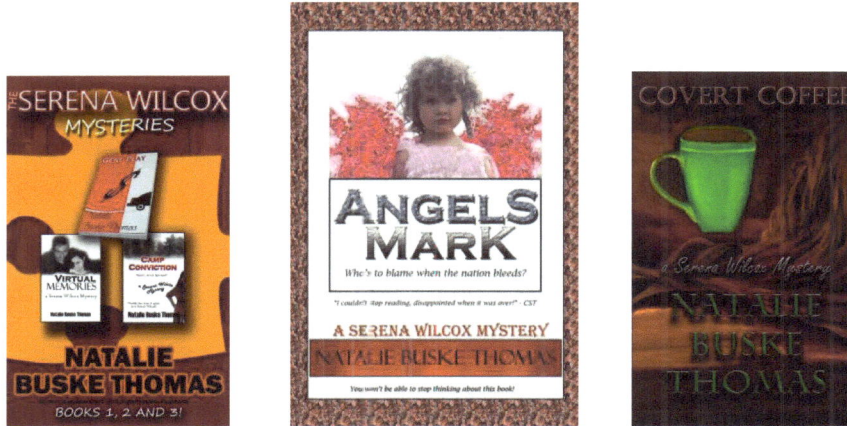

The Serena Wilcox Mysteries

Gene Play, Virtual Memories, Camp Conviction, Angels Mark, Covert Coffee

Juvenile fiction:

The Magic Camera

Non-fiction:

Fred Born Gifted

The Miracle Dulcimer

Oil paintings:

Savannah Reading in the Butterfly Garden

Life Sustaining

Ron and Joy before the War

Covert Coffee

Samples, excerpts, and oil paintings:

 www.nataliebuskethomas.com

Table of Contents:

Section 1:

The Miracle Dulcimer

The story behind the Miracle Dulcimer

We had taken up playing music together as a family. Sometimes we performed at senior centers, nursing homes or church services. My husband was making musical instruments for the kids because he had caught the music bug – an exciting new world of music and instruments had led to "I bet I could make these." And he could, beautifully!

Mom, who had never played an instrument before in her life and had never expressed a desire to learn, suddenly wanted a dulcimer like the one I was learning how to play. The problem was: Mom was very ill. She was in the final stages of COPD. She was so weak that she could barely hold a fork, and she was suffering from short term memory loss.

Even if my husband succeeded in making a beautiful instrument for her quickly, how could we then teach her how to play it? Mom was not known for having loads of patience. I needed a way for her to play music *instantly*, without the need for sheet music – she didn't know the first thing about how to read music – and without the need for practice. I wanted her to play music right away. Besides the lack of patience, time was not on our side.

We needed a way to make it happen and we created one. We hadn't given it a name at the time, nor did we think we'd ever do anything more with the idea. At the time it was a desperate attempt to help Mom play music, but the results of it were nothing short of a miracle: Mom played music for the first, and ast, time in her life. We brought our instruments to her apartment that afternoon, my husband, I and our three children. We all played simple songs together and Mom was able to play all of them. The moment that is forever etched in my mind is when we played Mom's favorite hymn "Amazing Grace". She didn't miss a single note.

I think somewhere in our hearts we knew it was to be our only window of opportunity, and that's why my husband was able to make such a beautiful dulcimer so quickly, and how I was inspired to create a method for playing it without any instruction, practice, or traditional sheet music. I thank God that He showed us a way to give her (and us) that moment. Few things in life are perfect and few relationships have fairy-tale endings. Closure was not easy for Mom and me. Playing music together did something for us that words could not. I want to share the Miracle Dulcimer with anyone who needs it – paying it forward, making a difference, whatever you want to call it. I know I can't let this divine intervention end with Mom and us.

This book contains instruction on how to convert your own dulcimer into a "Miracle Dulcimer" by simply using color coded numbers on the dulcimer itself and the song book included in this book. You may also convert any simple song once you get the hang of it (songs need to be simple so that the dulcimer can be played with only one finger on the string). My husband makes beautiful handcrafted dulcimers and he does take custom orders, although he will likely have to turn customers away at some point. Don't worry, you can find a similar instrument to what he makes fairly easily. Please refer to the section about what type of dulcimer this book is intended for before you shop for a dulcimer.

You may be wondering how this method of color-coded stickers is different from similar methods for learning how to play instruments. The difference between a child's beginning instrument and the Miracle Dulcimer is that a real instrument is used (not a plastic, cheap or inferior instrument that sounds horrible, which is often the case!), and the object is not to teach the music. The labels are with only one purpose in mind: *playing songs instantly*.

The joy that comes from playing music is difficult to describe, and there's no denying that it's therapeutic to play music. But if you or a loved one has physical limitations and/or a learning disability, or you/they are simply too impatient to put the hours into learning how to play an instrument (and perhaps more tedious, learning how to read sheet music) this is an excellent option for you.

Are there other books out there that show you how to play the dulcimer instantly? If there are, I couldn't find any when I needed them. I found many great resources for learning learn how to play the dulcimer, but for many people (like my mom), learning how to play an instrument is simply not realistic.

My method is not anything fancy or extraordinary – it is really just about the work of converting songs into numbers only (no sheet music) in simple arrangements (one string only) which I have done for you. Labeling the frets is nothing new, but I hadn't seen anyone doing this with adult instruments (Why not? Why make life so hard?). I provided you with instructions for how to label your dulcimer.

The Miracle Dulcimer method is ideal for hospice patients, special needs children or adults, young children, disabled persons, or anyone who has a desire to play music but is held back by the learning process. My husband would especially love to help disabled veterans play music. Because the ground work is done for you, you might consider starting small groups who would benefit from playing music together. Dulcimers are relatively inexpensive instruments – sponsors should be easy to find if your group doesn't have enough instruments to go around.

Maybe you just want to enjoy music without putting in the time or hassle. Some people never learn to play music because the process of learning how to play the instrument and read sheet music is too intense. Whatever your reason for wanting to play music instantly, I hope this book helps you.

If your reason for needing the Miracle Dulcimer is grief related, the following personal story may give you comfort. Feel free to move on to Section 2 if you prefer to dig right into the Miracle Dulcimer material.

The metal cabinet had to go – now, today. It had been a thorn in my side for years. It was an old horizontal filing cabinet with three large drawers that were hard to open and hard to close. It was a garish blue. Previous owners had graffiti-ed it up a little and then left it behind when they moved out of the house they sold us. The reason behind the abandonment of the blue filing cabinet was clear as soon as we tried to move it: heavy and cumbersome, this thing wasn't going anywhere.

I remember being seven months pregnant with our second child and surveying the state of our new home. It featured pet feces in the laundry area, light fixtures with all the light bulbs removed, and an un-flushed toilet. I had to clean the bathroom before any of us could use it.

Property left behind was also problematic, and it was tempting to leave it for the next homeowner to deal with. But because we believe that we are to always leave a place better than we found it, we moved the filing cabinet with us when we bought a new house. I had talked myself into perceiving the cabinet to be useful. I covered it with decorative decals to improve the look of it. And with great physical strain and emotional stress, the cabinet was hauled down the narrow stairs, out the door. I wanted the cabinet out of our hair and planned to sell it or give it away, whichever it came down to.

But I foolishly told my mother about this plan and she objected. The filing cabinet was handy, she said. Was I sure I wanted to get rid of it? Where would I put the kids' school things that I stored in there? Well, if I didn't want it, she said she wanted it. She lived on the third story of an apartment building. Thankfully it had an elevator, but even so, it was a heavy job to say the least. I fretted about the safety of my husband, Brent, and his agreeable helper.

While I'm often the one on the other side of "grab this end" heavy-lifting, this was definitely beyond my capabilities, and by that I mean more so than the usual "beyond". It was flat out impossible. Like most people, I judge possibilities for others based on my own limitations. I was quite anxious about the moving of this filing cabinet. I envisioned my husband throwing his back out, or crushing his arm between the cabinet and the wall – any manner of injuries could happen. Even death! What if the cabinet fell on Brent or his friend? Oh surely this wasn't worth doing!

And yet here we were; the filing cabinet was still our problem. Mom had died two days ago and we were cleaning out her apartment. I could barely stand to look at the cabinet, the cabinet Mom had crammed full of all manner of useful things. If we wanted tape or labels, she kept a lifetime (apparently greater than lifetime) supply in the cabinet. Wrapping paper? Rubber bands? Seven boxes of staples? Generc batteries purchased in bulk from eBay? What do you need? The cabinet was Mom's thrift shop where we could help ourselves to whatever we needed. And now she was gone.

Life goes on, I know that. I believe in heaven, God, angels, and good in general. But even the faithful need a sign sometimes. Cleaning out Mom's apartment was one of the worst experiences of my life and in the midst of it all I felt compelled to find a new home for the blue filing cabinet. Brent said he could bring it to our house if we couldn't get rid of it, but I was absolutely up-and-down convinced that if we put the cabinet out in the hallway with a "free" sign on it, someone would take it. And it had to be now. Brent didn't know quite how to handle me during this time of grief, so his best course of action was to do whatever I wanted. He helped me drag the cabinet out into the hallway.

Brent left shortly afterward on a food run. Alone, I was lost in a sea of dark thoughts. But not for long; someone was at the door. It was a woman asking if I was willing to hold the cabinet for her daughter. She thought her daughter would love having the use of the cabinet to store her sewing supplies. Of course I would hold the cabinet for her! I was amazed that my compulsion to put the cabinet in the hall had already proven to have merit. This being a senior apartment building, we seldom saw anyone under the age of 65 in the halls, so Brent's reservation that we wouldn't find a taker for the cabinet was a realistic concern.

Later, her daughter came to look at the cabinet. She loved it and thanked me several times. She couldn't believe her good fortune to have a perfect fit for her needs – completely free! Didn't I want anything for it? No, no I didn't. For not only did she already give me what I wanted, which was to be free of the cabinet, but she had also given me something else that she was completely unaware of.

She had arrived at my Mom's door with her beautiful newborn baby in her arms. It was the first time I'd ever seen a baby on the third floor of the senior apartment building. Mom's floor was especially quiet. It was most unexpected to see such a young baby – he couldn't be more than a couple days old. I was enchanted with her son upon first sight. I so wanted to touch him, but I didn't dare ask if I could. The magnetism of the babe was so strong that a revelation hit me. I asked her when her baby was born, although I was certain I already knew the answer. Yes, her baby was born on the same day that my mother died. As one exited, another entered. There was my sign, in this beautiful baby whose life was just beginning – life goes on.

I continue to find meaning in loss. What Mom and I went through can make a difference in the lives of other people. The Miracle Dulcimer method that I came up with in the middle of our crisis is something born of our experience, something of Mom. If people benefit from what happened to us, Mom lives on. Please open your heart and mind to the miracle of playing music.

Section Two:

How to Use This Book

Flip through the whole book if you haven't already. Since you are here on Section Two, you have probably already read (or skimmed) Section One, the introduction to this book. When you flip through the rest of the material, you will see that there are practical sections about the dulcimer itself (Section 3) and how to play it (Section 4), as well as personal stories and information about how to start a social group to regularly play music (Section 5). None of the information in sections 1-5 is necessary to read if you are in the position of "just give me what I need – NOW, please!"

If you are in a hurry, please head straight to Section 6: The Miracle Dulcimer Method. You'll also need the Appendix (to cut out the letters for labeling your dulcimer). Those two sections will get you what you most need to start playing music right away.

Sections 7-10 are loaded with songs you can play. I suggest you use a music stand to hold the book open while you play at a level that is easy to see while playing. To keep the book open to the page you want, use clothespins or clips if necessary. If you are playing at a table, or in a low seating position (such as when in a wheelchair) you might prefer to use a coffee table, end table, folding tray table, etc., and a cookbook stand – something along these lines. In other words, find a book holder solution that will keep the song pages at eye-level while playing.

This book has dozens of ready-to-play songs that will keep you entertained for a good long time. Some of the songs are more difficult than others, and longer, so you can grow into those when you are ready. All are common, familiar, popular tunes that most people already know the words to. It is much easier to play these songs if the only information on the page is the numbers for playing the song. Except for the gospel section, the songs are listed as numbers only, no lyrics. If you need lyrics for the other sections, it will be easy for you to find words to these common songs in an online search.

As a supplement to this book, you may view my how-to-play demonstration videos online for free. The videos teach different techniques for how to press the strings of the dulcimer, what a slide looks like (a slide is not necessary, but some prefer the sound of it and/or prefer to avoid finger soreness caused by direct contact with the strings), and other tips. Sometimes seeing an instrument demonstrated and played is helpful. You are invited to view the videos at www.nataliebuskethomas.com

Section Three:

Buying a Dulcimer and Accessories

I've already explained that my husband Brent made my mother's dulcimer. He can take a few custom orders, but he can't crank them out very quickly, and ordering from us (www.thomasfamilyartists.com) is not a realistic solution for everyone who needs a dulcimer. I will help you learn how to shop for a dulcimer that will work well with the labels and songbook that I created for Mom.

To use the Miracle Dulcimer method as described in this book you need a common mountain dulcimer with 4 strings (the first two are placed very close together, the other two are spread a bit farther apart) tuned to DAD tuning, the tuning recommended for beginners. Anyone who knows a thing or two about dulcimers would be able to point you to the basic instrument, and would also know what DAD tuning means, so please don't feel that you have to become an expert on the instrument before getting your hands on one.

Tuning an instrument can be a pesky chore. Honestly, I seldom tune my dulcimer – it sounds fine for a long time in my opinion, although before performing for others I make sure the dulcimer is tuned. If you are donating a dulcimer to someone else and can't check on the instrument, tuning the dulcimer frequently might not be something to worry about. It depends on how much of a musician's ear the person has, and how much it might bother them if the instrument is not perfectly in tune. I say all of this because someone who is struggling to play an instrument might find it taxing to tune it, and I'd hate for the love of playing to be thrown by the wayside because the instrument has fallen out of tune.

What if you can't tune it, or aren't around enough to tune it? Eventually the instrument will need to be tuned. An ongoing arrangement to tune the dulcimer might be a good plan, especially if the dulcimer is donated to, say, a nursing home, and you want the instrument to be ready for use at all times. I propose this solution: What a great volunteer opportunity for music students! Tuning is something they need to do routinely for their own instruments and they would be able to learn how to tune your dulcimer quickly, especially if they have experience in tuning other stringed instruments. Try calling schools and churches to find volunteers.

Other than the number of strings and frets, I do think it's important that you like the look of the instrument. The beauty of it, and how it feels in your hands, will add to or distract from the enjoyment of playing it. Musician's Friend (http://www.musiciansfriend.com/dulcimers) offers new dulcimers for reasonable prices. If you look around I'm sure you can find bargains elsewhere, and used dulcimers for even less. Dulcimers are a great choice for a low-cost instrument to get people of all income levels playing music. You can even make one yourself from a kit.

If you can afford to splurge a little, hand-crafted and specialty dulcimers are sold by many woodworkers, family-owned businesses (like ours: www.thomasfamilyartists.com) and artisans, but naturally you will have to pay more for a hand-crafted instrument than for an instrument that is factory made. Yet you might find it worth the expense due to the one-of-a-kind beauty of the instrument, especially if you are interested in the dulcimer as a gift for a loved one, or as a new healing, stress-release pastime for yourself. There is something about the look and feel of a beautifully crafted instrument that enriches the whole experience.

Once you have your dulcimer, here are some accessories you might want to add:

1. A strap to prevent the dulcimer from falling off your lap while playing (you can have some fun with this because the straps can be full of personality, pretty, colorful, etc.)
2. A flexible rubbery mat (square potholders work well) to put on your lap so that the dulcimer doesn't slide around while you play
3. Picks (the kind with a groove for a thumb-grip are easier to hold)
4. A slide (usually a small wooden dowel) Try a search for "pick and slide for mountain dulcimer"
5. A stand to hold your music/songbook (we like the heavy-duty kind with a solid back so that it's not top-heavy or easy to tip over – described as a deluxe, heavy-duty, or conductor's stand)
6. A tray table or other similar small table if playing the instrument on the lap is not desired (or not possible)
7. A tuner (if you don't know how to tune an instrument, you can get help for this at music stores – Once you understand how, you can use an online or phone app for tuning, or purchase a tuner)
8. A book or resource (DVD, CD, etc.) about the dulcimer

Section Four:

How to Play the Dulcimer

The dulcimer is played by pressing on the strings with one hand while strumming the strings with the other hand. Gifted musicians create chords and move their hands all over the strings, creating wonderful and complex arrangements.

This is not what I'm teaching you! Here, you'll only be concerned with ONE string. Press the first string (the string closest to you when you are holding the dulcimer). Strum the others. That's it. You can play the basic melody using this method. That will be enough for you or your loved one to experience playing music, especially if singing along with the tune or accompanied by other musicians or singers.

I created several videos to teach people how to play the dulcimer the easiest way possible, by using only the first string (ignore all the other strings). Feel free to view these videos and pass the link along to anyone else who might benefit. The link is on my website:

www.nataliebuskethomas.com

Section Five:

Being Social with your Dulcimer

It was still as glass on a frigid Minnesota night, ten degrees below zero. The full moon cast light over the snow and ice covered country road in front of an old small white church where the bluegrass group was gathered. My family and I had little experience with bluegrass music, but our son was so keenly interested in playing both guitar and harmonica that we dropped by one of their public events one day, and found them so welcoming that we kept turning up for their weekly bluegrass jams.

Our son gained valuable music experience from playing with other people. Veteran musicians were generous with their coaching and advice, so much so that they often talked over each other to have a turn at our budding musician. One thing led to another, and the rest of us wished we could join in. That's how we drifted toward playing musical instruments: once we sat in on a number of social gatherings, we wanted to be included in the fun.

I strongly recommend that you join a group or start your own – the benefits go way beyond becoming a better dulcimer player. Word of mouth and light advertising through community channels is probably all you need to do to get a small group going. Musicians love having a regular place to play and once they discover your group you are likely to get a regular jam session going quickly (while an all-dulcimer group would be interesting, I'm assuming you'll attract guitarists and other stringed-instrument musicians).

It's amazing what talent might be lying in your community waiting for an invitation. The group we were a part of eventually started performing at community events, which is something you may want to consider doing as well. However, your group might not have an interest in performing; create or find a group that fits your needs. The focus of your group might be casual playing and socializing. No matter how or why you form a group, the benefits are worthwhile.

You (or your loved one) will play better with encouragement and coaching from veteran musicians (musicians can't seem to resist helping each other, and old-timers like to help newbies). Your music will sound so much richer when other instruments (and voices) are joining in. Playing live music in a group is exciting!

Whether playing in a casual jam session or performing for a community event, cookies and coffee are often served either midway through the event or afterward. People naturally gravitate toward food and chatting after playing music together. The social benefits are hard to measure: your life will be richer when playing music with other people. Regularly playing music with others could open a whole new world for someone who is lonely, bored, or simply open to expanding one's horizons.

Please consider organizing a group for playing music together on a regular basis. All you need is a place to play and someone willing to lead. Here are 10 tips for organizing an "all skill levels welcome" group:

1. **Invite seasoned musicians** to join you; not necessarily dulcimer players – a wide range of instruments creates a rich sound. Beginning students will enjoy the experience of playing exciting live music right away, even if they can only play the basic melody line.
2. **Play easy songs for the first half of the session**. I suggest you use the songs in this book so that your beginning players can participate. Experienced musicians are good sports about playing simple songs to help beginning musicians.
3. Keep a **slow pace while playing, but a fast transition time between songs**. Allow players to play at a slow tempo, and repeat the songs through several verses. You may choose to allow a couple verses as solos, moving around the room. However, when changing from song to song, keep the group moving – minimize the chatting between songs. Players who are excited to play music will become frustrated if chatter and delays between songs cause the session to lag. You don't want your players sitting around not playing music!
4. At the end of the easy-play half, **take a break for chatting and snacking**. This is an opportunity for folks to contribute favorite goodies, serve coffee etc. Sometimes non-players enjoy providing this for the group; if invited, people will come to watch and become "the audience" – they often join in by singing, especially if you provide them with the song lyrics.
5. How long should the first half be? Anywhere from 30 minutes to 60 minutes, even 90 minutes! **"About an hour" is a good rule of thumb, and keeping on a schedule is a good idea for all.** However, if the session is sputtering along with few players, you might want to wrap up at the half hour mark. If you are having a wonderful session and you can tell that folks are "just getting started", by all means, let them play longer. If you've gone over your planned hour, do reel them in at the 90 minute mark. Some players will secretly be weary of playing and will be relieved that you've ended the session – others might be hungry, thirsty or in need of a restroom break! Sometimes people don't know when to quit, so make sure that the person leading the group (you?) ends the first half in a friendly but firm way.

6. Now it's time to **socialize! Eat, drink; be merry!** Coffee and desserts are usually what people serve. Sessions are typically held in church basements or community rooms. I have never seen alcohol served at these functions and I strongly suggest that you don't allow it, especially if children might be attending. You never know when alcohol might be a problem for one or more of your members. We have wrapped sessions around a potluck dinner and that was enjoyable as a special occasion "bonus" gathering. Food really brings people together so I hope you will include feeding your members as a regular part of these music sessions.

7. For **the second half of your session, let the experienced musicians lead** (assuming you have at least two advanced players; if not, coffee/snack time is a good place to stop). Musicians can select songs from their own song books, take song requests from the group or audience members, etc. Musicians sometimes bring copies of music so that everyone can join in – a courteous gesture and a real treat.

   Encourage beginners to strum along even if they don't know the song and can't keep up; watching or singing is also fine. Your musicians will enjoy this part of the session and some will grab the spotlight on occasion. This is okay, as long as you keep a watch on the time and allow equal spotlight amongst all who want it. People might do a bit of storytelling also, and as long as this doesn't run on too long, this too is welcome. It's helpful to have at least one leader of the group who will keep things moving along without any hard feelings. It is helpful to **open the session with a few ground rules so that folks know what to expect and don't take things personally when the group leader moves things along**.

8. Finally, as the second hour closes, you can **close the session with a few words and give any announcements about upcoming sessions**. You can then **invite folks to stay and jam** as long as they'd like. At this point people move about the room. Some re-arrange chairs to create smaller groups, others gather to socialize a bit more. Many say their good-byes and leave right away. Sometimes impromptu teaching/coaching/mentoring happens. If there's no reason to shoo people out, some might stay and play music late into the night (if this is acceptable).

9. You can **decide as a group if you want to do any public performances, as well as appoint a substitute group leader** in the event that you (or whoever is leading) can't make it to a session, or need to leave the session early. Leading and organizing the group shouldn't be taxing, but a little bit of leadership and organization will help things run smoothly for all.

10. Lastly, you should **consider what you will and won't allow**. Are children invited? If so, what ages? What plan do you have if the children are disruptive (creating a stressful environment for those seeking music for therapy)? Are there any instruments not allowed? For example, some groups don't allow percussion. Some groups have no guidelines and just let the musicians gather with whatever instruments they have. Others request "stringed instruments only". Others don't restrict the group to stringed instruments, but due to performing while seated in a group circle, pianos, drum sets, etc. are not allowed. Shakers, tambourines, and other non-stringed hand-held instruments are sometimes allowed.

Section Six:

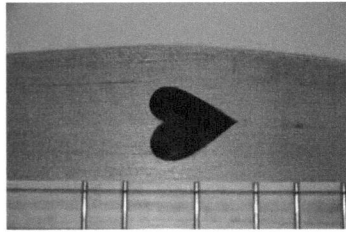

The Miracle Dulcimer Method

Now that you've learned about the dulcimer, and what you might like to do with it, you are ready to give it a go! The "Miracle Dulcimer" method will allow you or a loved one to play music instantly. Just cut out the letters from the back pages of this book and apply them to your dulcimer with removable glue dots (inexpensive) or something similar (choose a substance you can remove later, without ruining the finish on your dulcimer, unless you are sure that you want the letters to stay on forever). Alternatively you can purchase small letter stickers to apply to your dulcimer.

Another way to apply letters is to place the letter on the instrument and tape over the letter with clear packing tape – it will seal the letter in and adhere it to the instrument. You are likely to ruin the finish on the instrument if you want to remove the packaging tape later, so don't do this unless you are completely sure that you don't want to remove the letters later on down the road.

After you have placed the letters on the instrument according to the diagram (also found in the back of this book, with the letters) you are ready to play songs!

1. Remember to press the first string (the first two strings are close together and count as one string, press down on BOTH). You can use your finger or a slide (most people use a small wooden dowel if using a slide).
2. Strum the other end of the dulcimer with your fingers or a pick (most people prefer using a pick).
3. Just follow along with the letters in the song (one hand pressing the string near the correct fret), the other hand strumming).
4. A zero means NO STRING is pressed (that's called "open string"). Don't press the strings, but DO continue strumming. The numbers refer to the lines on the dulcimer (the frets). The first fret is 1, the second fret a 2, etc. (going from left to right down the neck).
5. Double-digit numbers are underlined so that you know the difference between 10 (one and a zero) and <u>10</u> (ten), or 11 (two ones) and <u>11</u> (eleven), for example.

Section Seven: Songbook #1

Children's Songs

Twinkle Twinkle Little Star

3377887 6655443

7766554 7766554

3377887 6655443

Rain, Rain Go Away

75 775 7758 775

Mary Had a Little Lamb

5434555 444 577

5434555 544543

The Farmer in the Dell

033333   455555

778753   455443

This Old Man

757   757   8765456

567   333   34567

744   6543

Are You Sleeping, Brother John

3453   3453   567   567

787653   787653

303   303

Old Mac Donald

3330110 55443

0 3330110 55443

00 333 00333 333 333

333333 3330110 55443

Section Eight: Songbook #2

Christmas Songs

Away in a Manger

77655 433210

00100 421035

77655 433210

065454 34123

Silent Night

7875 7875

11 11 9   10 10 7

88 10 98 7875

88 10 98 7875

11 11 13 11 9 10 12

10 757643

O Come All Ye Faithful

330340   545654

032 1234   52100

76565 453421 0

3323430 5545654

56543236   5433

O Christmas Tree

0333   4555   5456243

0333   4555   5456243

77587766   66476655

0333   4555   5456243

We Wish You a Merry Christmas

03343211   14454320

05565431   001423

Jingle Bells

05430 0005431

16541 77645

05430 05431

11654777 7875437

555 555 57345

666 6655 555 44547

555 555 57345

666 6655 5577643

The Little Drummer Boy

0 0 1 2 2 2 2 2 32 3 2 22 2 22

0 0 1 2 2 2 2 32 32 2 22 2 22

1 2 3 4 4 4

5 43 2 1 11 1 11

1 2 3 4 4 4 5 65 4 3 33

54 3 2 22 43 2 1 11 1 11

0 0 1 2 2 2 2 32 32 2 22 2 22

10 1 0 00 0 00

Section Nine: Songbook #3

Gospel Songs

Amazing Grace

03535 4310

Amazing grace how sweet the sound

03535 47

That saved a wretch like me

575753 013310

I once was lost, but now I'm found

03 5543

Was blind, but now I see

Will the Circle Be Unbroken

01   33 543 5

Will the circle be unbroken

54   31   3   1   0

By and by, Lord, by and by

01   33   56   75

There's a bet-ter home a'waitin'

345   3 443

In the sky, Lord, in the sky

Alternate lyrics to same tune:

So re-mem-ber Our Defen-der
Died for us and rose a-ga-in
For He is our loving Sav-ior
And a Joy that has no end

What a Friend We Have in Jesus

7 7 8 7 5 3 3 1

What a friend we have in Je-sus,

Have we tri-als and temptations?

0 3 5 3 7 5 4

All our sins and griefs to bear!

Is there trou-ble a-nywhere?

7 7 8 7 5 3 3 1

What a priv-i-lege to car-ry,

We should ne-ver be dis-cour-aged;

0 3 5 4 3 2 3

Ev-'ry thing to God in prayer!

Take it to the Lord in prayer.

4 3 4 5 6 4 5 7 8 8 7 5 6 5 4

What a peace we of-ten for-feit. What a need-less pain we bear.
Can we find a friend so faith-ful who will all our sor-rows share?

7 7 8 7 5 3 3 1 0 3 5 4 3 2 3

All be-cause we do not car-ry ev-'ry-thing to God in prayer.
Jesus knows our ev-ery weak-ness; take it to the Lord in prayer.

In the Garden

0 0 2 3 0 3 4 5

I come to the garden alone

He speaks and the sound of His voice,
I'd stay in the garden with Him

4333343 30

While the dew is still on the roses

Is so sweet the birds hush their singing
Tho' the night around me be falling

23442 12345

And the voice I hear, falling on my ear

And the melody that He gave to me
But He bids me go, throu' the voice of woe

5454   3234

The Son of God discloses

Within my heart is ringing
His voice to me is calling

54333 21222 00666545

& He walks with me & He talks with me & He tells me I am his own

34554 42333 1033243

And the joy we share as we tarry there, None other has ever known

I Love to Tell the Story

0 3 00 3 5 4 3 3 3 1 4 3 1 0

I love to tell the sto-ry Of un-seen things a-bove,

I love to tell the story; More wonderful it seems

I love to tell the story; 'Tis pleasant to repeat

I love to tell the story, For those who know it best

0 4 3 4 5 4 3 3 5 7 5 5 4 3 4

Of Je-sus and His glo-ry, Of Je-sus and His love.

Than all the golden fancies Of all our golden dreams.

What seems, each time I tell it, More wonderfully sweet.

Seem hungering and thirsting To hear it, like the rest,

4 4 56 6 6 5 5 5 43 43 2

I love to tell the sto-ry; Be-cause I know it's true;

I love to tell the story; It did so much for me,

I love to tell the story, For some have never heard

And when in scenes of glory I sing the new, new song,

2 1 23 11 0 3 4 35 4 3

It sat-is-fies my long-ings As no-thing else can do.

And that is just the reason I tell it now to thee

The message of salvation From God's own Holy Word

'Twill be the old, old story That I have loved so long.

Doxology

3 3 2 1 0 3 4 5

Praise God, from whom all bless-ings flow;

5 5 5 3 6 5 4

Praise Him all creatures here be-low

3 4 5 4 3 1 2 3

Praise Him a-bove, ye Heaven'y host;

7 5 3 4 6 5 4 3

Praise Fa-ther, Son and Ho-ly Ghost

Section Ten: Songbook #4

Campfire & Sing-a-longs

Kum Ba Yah

35777 887

35777 654

35777 887

653443

Clementine

3330 5553 3577 654

4566 5453 3540243

On Top of Old Smokey

3357 **10** 8 86787

335774 56543

Michael Row the Boat Ashore

357 5787   5787

577 5654   34543

Oh! Susanna

34577 8753 455434

34577 8753 455443

6688   877534

34577 8753 455443

Red River Valley

035543 4313

035 357 654

7650 543 4576

1 1 0 234 543

This Land is Your Land

34566 63455

33544 443455

334566 663455

44420243

Appendix:

Diagram of dulcimer, Letters for labeling your dulcimer

The above picture is an example of how to place the numbers on the dulcimer. I suggest that you put them along the raised edge, on the side facing the musician while the instrument is played. Place the numbers close to the frets.

This dulcimer above is a left-handed dulcimer that was custom made for my mother (ignore the colors on hers, yours are labeled differently). In the next photo I'll show you a right-handed dulcimer.

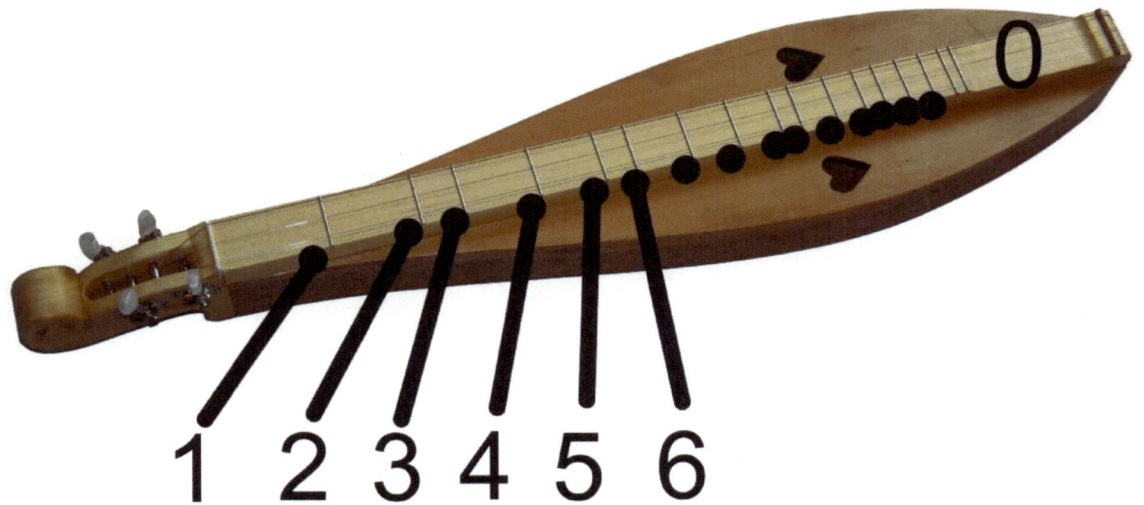

Notice the zero on the strumming area? It's called an "open string" when the music calls for strumming only, NO strings pressed. The strings are labeled just to the left of the frets, almost touching the frets, but not quite (the frets are the bars/lines). Some dulcimers have a 6 ½ fret. Others don't. Make sure that you ask when you buy your dulcimer if you aren't sure.

If you have a 6 ½ fret, the numbering is like this:
1 2 3 4 5 6 6.5 7 8 9 10 11 12 etc.
These easy-play songs don't use the 6.5 fret, so you'll skip that one (don't label it with anything) and move on to the next fret for 7.

If you don't have a 6 ½ fret on your dulcimer, your numbering is like this:
1 2 3 4 5 6 7 8 9 10 11 12 etc.
If you don't have a 6 ½ fret, you won't need to skip a fret between 6 and 7.

If you don't understand what I mean by the 6 ½ fret ask your dulcimer salesperson. Don't forget to skip the fret between #6 and #7 if you are labeling a dulcimer that has a 6 ½ fret.

Some songs use that extra note, but you don't need to worry about that for the songs in this book. You also don't need to worry about the high notes.

Here are the numbers you can cut out to place on your dulcimer.

Removable glue dots or something similar should work well for you. I'll give you two sets n case you make a mistake while cutting them out. You have permission to copy this page and modify the numbers in any way that you need.

1	2	3	4	5	6
7	8	9	10	11	12
13					

1	2	3	4	5	6
7	8	9	10	11	12
13					

I hope this book has helped you.
Please feel free to contact me with your personal stories.

Natalie Buske Thomas author/artist web site: www.nataliebuskethomas.com
Thomas Family web site: www.thomasfamilyartists.com
Twitter: @writernbt
Facebook: Natalie Buske Thomas
Pinterest: writernbt

www.ingramcontent.com/pod-product-compliance
Lightning Source LLC
Chambersburg PA
CBHW041427090426
42741CB00002B/68